INCOMERS t

Helen Harris

Peninsula
Press

First published in 2007 by Peninsula Press,
an imprint of Forest Publishing
Woodstock
Liverton
Newton Abbot
Devon TQ12 6JJ

British Library Cataloguing in Publication Data

A catalogue record for this book is available from the British Library.

ISBN 978–1–872640–56–3

Editorial, design and layout by:
Mike Lang

Typeset by:
Carnaby Typesetting, Torquay, Devon TQ1 1EG

Printed and bound in Great Britain by:
Wotton Printers Limited, Newton Abbot, Devon TQ12 4PJ

CONTENTS

Acknowledgements

My thanks are due to the following for help and information received during the preparation of this work:–

Mr Paul Clarke (Bradworthy Parish Council) and Mrs Daphne Nicholls (Bradworthy Museum); Mr Russell Woolcock; Mr Robert Lush and Miss Jane Evans (Tiverton Museum); Mr Stuart Barker (Buckfastleigh Town Council); Mr Lee Hiscock (Corporate Information Services, Devon County Council); Mr Martin Turner (Centre for Rural Research, University of Exeter); Westcountry Studies Library.

I have also referred to Mike Sampson's *A History of Tiverton* (2004) for certain details.

Introduction

In May 2006 the History Section of the Devonshire Association, of which I am an active member, held a seminar at Exeter University under the title 'Raiders and Invaders'. The Romans, the Vikings, and Pirates were the subjects of the first three lectures, and I was asked to consider the modern, more friendly, phenomenon of Incomers.

I began by asking members of the 140-strong audience to raise their hands if: 1, they had been born in Devon, and 2, 3 and 4 if both their parents, and successively four grandparents, and eight great-grandparents had been born in the county. It could be seen that rather fewer than half had hands up for 1, with diminishing numbers for 2 and 3, while only very few of us could declare that all our great-grandparents were Devonians. Whilst these revelations may or may not be representative of the total population of Devon today, they are at least an indication of a trend which is becoming increasingly apparent.

My study centred mainly on the migration of people to Devon from other parts of Britain rather than from abroad, because – at least up to the present day – it is mainly from here that the movement has come. Compared with some other counties, Devon has few incomers from other continents and countries. Several come from distant parts of the world on a temporary basis, for example to study at our universities, or to work with firms established from overseas, or to fill seasonal jobs, but few remain as permanent residents. And it seems that in the recent past people have not come in appreciable numbers from other countries of Europe.

Until the end of the eighteenth century there was generally very little movement of people except within their own country areas. By the middle of the nineteenth century, despite considerable migrations to London and the developing industrial towns, more than half of people in England and Wales were still living in the counties in which they had been born. During the twentieth century Devon's population rose by more than 50 per cent – from approximately 662,000 in 1901 to over one million by 2001. Devonians are normally prolific, but not exceptionally so, and many younger people move away to seek fortunes elsewhere, so the increase is clearly due to the number of incomers who have taken up residence in the county.

What have been the reasons for so many people coming to Devon in the past century or so?

In my consideration of this question four main reasons have emerged. People have come to Devon for land; for industry; to take up jobs and appointments; and for retirement (also, of course, many have come on

A map of Devon showing the places featured in this study.

marriage to established Devonians). In studying these reasons I have focused on four locations, in different parts of the county, as typical examples. These places are, however, but examples; similar methods of study may be applied to countless others.

Taking into account the evidence of the 'show of hands' exercise noted above, the chances are that readers of this are more likely than not to be 'new', or second generation, rather than 'native' Devonians. Where that is so, incomers' individual experiences will, for them, add personal interest to the study.

Helen Harris

April 2007

CHAPTER ONE

Incomers for land

The quest for land is without doubt the earliest of reasons for the advance of people from other parts to the area we now know as Devon. From 'time beyond mind' waves of immigrants have come to seek a livelihood – from prehistoric settlers to Romans, Vikings, Normans and many others. Some later retreated, others stayed, or at least left their genes amongst the slowly growing population.

Similar aspirations prompted comparable movements in the years immediately following the Second World War. In the late 1940s and early 1950s large numbers of people were being discharged from HM Forces, many of whom had no previous jobs to which they could return. Apart from the modest gratuity payments, many found themselves with only limited means. As young couples and families were reunited the need for income became imperative, and some considered farming. At the same time, with the resumption of peace, developments in the growth of essential housing, industry, roads and airports were taking place throughout the country, particularly in the South East, and this meant that many farming people were required to forsake their land as modernisation swept in. Those enhanced by wartime government aid in the need for home-produced food, and by compensation for their uprooting, could consider a wide range of possibilities for relocation, including the richer farming parts of Devon. For those short of capital, however, Devon held attractions for other reasons – in certain districts land was very cheap.

The tract of Culm Measures, which extends across north-west Devon eastwards from the Cornish border and north of Dartmoor, has always presented an inhospitable face to any seeking an easy living from the land. Heavy and acidic, and with an annual rainfall approaching 50 inches, this former moorland is conducive to the growth of rushes and other indigenous plants such as meadowsweet, hemp agrimony and ragwort. In the winter it can easily become waterlogged and must be grazed sparingly to avoid poaching. Nevertheless, its remoteness, wildness and open character, and the freshness of salty breezes that blow in across the Atlantic coast, provide a deep attraction for many, particularly in the long days of summer.

The war brought changes to this part of Devon, as elsewhere. With food production having become a priority, the Ministry of Agriculture was assigned wide powers concerning cultivations and management of the land, which were delegated to County War Agricultural Committees.

A corner of rush-infested, unimproved land in Bradworthy parish. (Author)

Devon was divided into eleven districts, based on market towns, each with its own committee of local farmers. Technical advice was made available to farmers, and financial help provided in the form of guaranteed prices and subsidies, and some of the more unfavourable land was brought into production. The ending of hostilities did not bring an immediate change: the world was short of food, and rationing continued in Britain for six more years. Moreover, due to the war-depleted state of the nation's economy, home agriculture continued to be of vital importance and was given every encouragement.

Devon's Culm Measures land is an area containing mainly small farms, offering fairly low subsistence livelihoods. Traditionally, the keeping of cattle and sheep had been the main activities, which more often than not included the growing of corn and root crops as well as the making of hay. Up to the time of the war cattle were mostly of the Red Devon beef breed, or crosses, from which surplus milk would be scalded for cream and butter making. But then, as the need for milk for human consumption and for manufacture increased, large numbers of these small farmers were recruited into milk selling by the large local creameries, regardless of the fact that conditions then existing on the farms were mainly unsuitable for dairying.

After the war many people who had 'hung on' during the difficult days,

Above and below: Improved grassland in Bradworthy parish, showing increased stocking potential. (Author)

perhaps having accumulated some modest financial resources, decided to progress to enhanced chances elsewhere, or to give up farming, maybe to retire to an attractive bungalow at Bude, or wherever. Thus, many of these small farms came on to the market at prices commonly amounting to about £200 per acre, or sometimes less – around £100 per acre was not unknown. For this the incomer might have a farm of say 30 indifferent acres, a house in need of repair and probably without electricity, unimproved farm buildings, and a doubtful well for water supply. The situation did, however, provide a roof overhead for those needing a home, and also – importantly – the opportunity to produce and sell milk.

Poor though the land might be, in most cases it had the potential for improvement. Help was at hand from the Ministry's agricultural advisers (who had become part of the National Agricultural Advisory Service [NAAS] in 1946) and was freely sought by the farmers. Drainage was a priority, including the clearing of ditches, and selective weedkillers were applied to eliminate the rushes. Later, ploughing and direct reseeding with preferred grass species, with suitable applications of lime and fertiliser, would usually produce a transformation. The operations were costly, but various government grants were available to assist. Once improved, and given careful management, very good grass for grazing could be produced, and silage making was generally adopted as the main means of conservation. Increased stocking rates were possible and parishes took on a new appearance. (This writer, in fact, found some difficulty in finding remaining examples of unimproved pasture to photograph for illustrative purposes.)

For some time milk producers were hampered by the unsuitability of their facilities. Vividly remembered are hot summers when farm wells ran dry so that there was inadequate (often polluted) water for washing dairy equipment properly, and cooling of the milk was impossible. Churns of milk would wait for collection on a stand at the farm entrance, in the warm sun. Sadly, but not surprisingly, the milk might then be sour on reaching the dairy, be rejected, and the churns returned the next day with red labels. Such losses were serious for the farmers who relied desperately on their monthly milk cheques, and the NAAS dairy adviser would be called in to try to help.

Following the introduction of new Milk & Dairies regulations in 1949, it became necessary for premises to be improved, with moves also towards the tuberculin testing of cows. Further advisory visits and necessary works proceeded through the 1950s (the worst cases were tackled first), by which time the advance of mains water and electricity was under way. In later years, however, due to changes in agricultural economics, many small dairy farmers have ceased production, perhaps with amalgamation of holdings, or have concentrated again on rearing beef cattle and sheep.

A typical parish on this type of land, which may be considered as an example, is Bradworthy. Located in the north-west of the county, it is reasonably remote, but with a strong community spirit. The land rises to 700ft, bordered on the west by the infant reach of the River Tamar, forming the Cornish boundary. The settlement is believed to date from c.720 AD, the village square – one of the largest in the Westcountry – and numerous hamlets scattered throughout the parish (often with names ending in 'worthy') being indications of Saxon settlement. The village is pleasant, and the parish has around 450 households, about three-quarters of them owner-occupied. This is one of the many areas of the kind already described, where 'adventurers' came in the mid-twentieth century to engage in farming. Some of them eventually abandoned the exercise, others stayed, and a few, having upgraded the standard of their farms, sold out to other incomers and moved on elsewhere.

As in most cases, the village of Bradworthy has seen new developments, including houses on the village fringes. Some light industries have been established on a small industrial estate, and three wind turbines were erected on high ground in the west in 2005. As regards the population, this

Bradworthy village square is one of the largest in the Westcountry. (Author)

Long-established village houses in Bradworthy. (Author)

Part of Bradworthy square, showing the church. (Author)

Modern housing on the Bradworthy village fringe. (Author)

Three wind turbines erected in Bradworthy parish in 2005. (Author)

was already relatively high in earlier centuries when agriculture was the main occupation, but it rose significantly towards the mid-nineteenth century as farming prospered, necessitating larger work forces, and with the prevalence of bigger families. Later, towards the mid-twentieth century, there followed a fall due to agricultural depression and then to increased mechanisation only for it to rise again, to over 1,000, at the start of the present century. Even in this fairly remote rural situation it is estimated locally that 30-40% of the present population are newcomers, with census migration figures indicating that the majority have come from London and south-east England, with a scattering from other places.

Population – Bradworthy

1801	1851	1901	1931	1961	2001
634	1,071	847	775	697	1,082

The community is very self-contained. Various tradesmen, such as motor vehicle repairers, joiners and plumbers, serve a wide surrounding area and the village has commendable shops. A factory producing hearing aids employs about fifty people, and there are providers of bed and breakfast, and a few holiday homes. There are around a hundred children in the village school.

Prices of agricultural land have, of course, risen substantially since those times of half a century ago. Even in 2007, when many farmers are having to struggle to make a living, the escalation continues. Buyers include incomers to Devon who see the business advantages, with the awareness that for inheritance purposes agricultural land qualifies for tax relief. There is, in fact, a shortage of land and farms, which makes the purchase of nearby land, for farmers wishing to expand, very expensive. For example, 30 acres of agricultural land just a few miles from Bradworthy, near Holsworthy, was sold very recently by tender for £3,500 per acre. Many of the buyers of farms in Devon, particularly incomers, will be prepared to pay a considerable sum in order to acquire a good farmhouse as a dwelling. They may then sell off most of the land, or let it. Land, like 'bricks and mortar', continues to be seen as a secure investment, preferred by many to stocks and shares.

The past half century has seen intense and increasing demands for land for building development and, where planning permission is granted, selling prices for land rise astronomically. All parts of Devon have been subject to structural expansion due to an increasing population, and the pressure continues. There is virtually no town or village in the county that has not spread out to absorb some of the surrounding countryside.

Many of the areas of development have hitherto been in agricultural production, and are attractive scenically. Those who care, therefore, feel sadness in considering green fields disappearing under masonry and tarmac. Such, however, are the pressures of today's world that now, after thousands of years, still the people come in their numbers, seeking land.

CHAPTER TWO

Incomers for industry

Devon has a long history of indigenous industries, based on its natural resources. Seas of the south and north coastlines have provided rich fishing grounds; Dartmoor and other locations with mineral deposits gave rise to mining. Most areas of the county have also been used for farming, with sheep an important enterprise and one that from the thirteenth century, aided by the availability of fast-flowing rivers and streams for washing and power, led to the traditional domestic processes of wool spinning and weaving being developed into a leading industry.

One place where, from the fifteenth century, great wealth was created by woollen manufacture and trade was Tiverton. Situated fourteen miles north of Exeter on the River Exe amid rich farming country, the town was founded as a royal estate in Saxon times, probably in the seventh century. Through succeeding centuries Tiverton grew as a market town and also developed industrially. The manufacture of woollen kersey became established under merchants who included John Greenway, John Waldron and Peter Blundell, and by the sixteenth century Tiverton was one of the leading markets for cloth in the West of England.

Towards the end of the eighteenth century, however, the woollen industry in Devon was seeing some decline, partly due to the development of manufacture in Yorkshire. As an intended solution for Tiverton, two of the cloth merchants, inspired by mechanical advances of the Industrial Revolution, decided, in the early l790s, to construct a new factory beside the Exe – for cotton. This was built on the west side of the river (where today's factory stands) and was powered by water brought from the river by a mile-long leat. By 1793 it was in use, although it appears that wool worsted cloth, rather than the envisaged cotton, was being produced. Difficulties ensued. Workers were not happy with the machines, fearing loss of jobs. And on the international scene, from 1789 until 1793, France was embroiled in civil revolution, which was followed (in 1793) by the beginning of Britain's long war with the French Republic. The effects of both were disastrous for Tiverton's already failing trade, and early in 1815 an auction of the five-storey factory – equipped for spinning and weaving – was being advertised.

Unrest at the development of machines in industry was felt not only at Tiverton. When the war ended in 1815 general discontent was being manifested more fiercely in other parts of the country, due to national debt caused by the conflict; this resulted in high taxes, the high price of bread,

The River Exe at Tiverton, showing the factory of John Heathcoat & Company and the outflow of the leat. (Author)

The east-bank view upstream from Exe Bridge, Tiverton. (Author)

and unemployment. Unemployment was felt particularly in the textile industry. The mechanisation of spinning had been developing for some years, and now power looms for weaving were also proliferating. With human skills tending to become redundant, protestors known as Luddites proceeded to attack mills and smash machinery in the Midlands as well as in Lancashire and Yorkshire.

At this time a skilled and highly intelligent young man called John Heathcoat was living in the Long Whatton-Hathern area of north Leicestershire. He was in partnership in a lace factory at nearby Loughborough. Born in 1783, the son of a Duffield (Derbyshire) farmer, Heathcoat had, in 1808, ingeniously invented and patented a bobbin-net (later known as plain net) machine which, using twisted cotton thread, enabled lace resembling the hand-made to be produced mechanically. By 1815 several of his machines were installed under licence at other factories, bringing him financial gain. However, probably motivated by experience of industrial jealousies as well as the Luddite risks, in 1815 he set his eyes on a more distant and reputedly peaceable location when he heard of the factory for sale at Tiverton. Towards the end of that year he journeyed to Tiverton and purchased the mill, and in the early part of 1816 was arranging for the installation of his machines. Such arrangements for establishment at Tiverton were timely for Heathcoat and his partner John Boden, as in June 1816 their Loughborough factory was attacked and the machines there were smashed.

Heathcoat's intention was to bring members of his workforce to Tiverton for partial staffing of the factory – initially around twenty skilled men to form a nucleus to train the many unemployed Tiverton people he planned to take on. These lacemakers, framesmiths and mechanics, who set out in the early summer and walked the 200 or so miles, could thus be said to have been among the earliest of Devon's 'incomers for industry'.

Most probably they made their way from Loughborough to Leicester and then along the straight Fosse Way down towards Devon, a journey that apparently took from seven to ten days. Other men, together with wives and families, followed later.

One wonders at the impressions of these incomers from Leicestershire as they reached their destination. In particular, wearied by their walking, they would have been well aware of the Westcountry hills and fast-flowing brooks – so different from the flatter land and more sluggish streams that they had left. They would have encountered the newly constructed Grand Western Canal as they neared Tiverton and probably remarked on the breadth of the River Exe as they crossed it on reaching the town. What would the town have been like? The population, given as 6,505 in 1801, was about a third of that today, but the dwellings were more crowded. Green fields would have been in evidence much closer to the urban area, and perhaps it would have brought some solace to the newcomers to see them grazed by the Red Devon cattle, which were not too different from the Longhorns and Shorthorns that stocked the land around Loughborough, where Robert Bakewell of Dishley Grange had worked in his pioneering of animal husbandry. Our ancient deep Devon hedgebanks would possibly have been a source of comment to those more accustomed to the slimmer lengths of quickthorn set for fencing in the recent activity of Parliamentary Enclosure – fences that were easy for Leicestershire hunts to jump over. How did they find the local people? Despite some differences of speech they would have had a common experience in the working of yarns; while the Devonians had grown up with the home spinning and weaving of wool, the incomers could compare the use in homes and workshops of cotton, wool and silk for framework knitting in the Midlands hosiery industry.

The initial party of workers from Leicestershire, and those who soon followed, represented the different skills and trades needed by John Heathcoat as he established his Tiverton lace factory. It is believed that the laceworkers and their families who came on foot numbered around 500. In addition, Heathcoat took into employment many others – from Tiverton and surrounding parishes, from distant parts of Devon and even from neighbouring counties. From an index of employees in contract of employment with the firm, workers' names, job descriptions, and often where they came from can be seen. Names of early arrivals from Leicestershire include: Swift (described as a framesmith), Yates, Lee, Soars, Craswell, Towndrow, Smith, and Squires, all of whom were given as lacemakers. Others follow through the long list, interspersed with many established local surnames. It is more than likely that some families living in Tiverton at the present time have surnames inherited from those incomers. Although some later moved away, it is presumed that the majority stayed on, doubtless marrying established Tivertonians, so an element of Leicestershire bloodlines must surely exist.

One family which is still well known in the area is that of John Heathcoat himself. John Heathcoat and his wife Ann (née Caldwell) had a son who died in infancy and also three daughters. In 1826 one of the daughters, also named Ann, married Samuel Amory, a London solicitor whom Heathcoat already held in a position of trust. Eventually it was their son, John Heathcoat Amory, who, taken as a partner into the family business (which had become John Heathcoat & Company in 1852), succeeded his grandfather on his retirement in 1859.

After his retirement, John Heathcoat lived just two more years – he died on 18 January 1861 aged 77. During his lifetime he had been responsible for

John Heathcoat, 1783 – 1861. (Courtesy of John Heathcoat & Company)

much building in Tiverton. In the early days he began acquiring land and built houses for the growing workforce which, besides men, included many women who were largely engaged in lace mending. He also took on children from the age of twelve and was generally regarded as a considerate employer. He extended buildings at the factory and also built a school at the factory gates, where mothers coming to work could leave their children; the building still stands, now housing the factory shop. Great developments took place in the Westexe area, with many dwellings set in 'courts'. Some of these opened from the street along Westexe South before they were swept away for the street widening in the late 1950s and replaced with council estates. (Impressive decorations in these courts at the times of twentieth century royal coronations and jubilee had been indications of a high level of national loyalty.)

On 5 December 1936 the original factory building suffered a serious fire, plunging the workpeople and others in Tiverton into a state of anxiety. It was, however, speedily rebuilt to suitable standards, and ready for use in 1938.

In the early twentieth century the firm had around 2,000 employees. The ringing of a bell signalled the beginning and end of work, and men and women in their scores would stream along surrounding streets leading to their houses. Diversification has been a key factor in maintaining business. Whilst the making of silk lace continued until 1982 many other processes have been introduced over the years. During the Second World War nylon parachutes were made, and currently many kinds of textile materials are produced, including gearing belts, car air bags, tarpaulins, nets for fish farming, safety garments and cot mattress covers. Much is exported. The workforce today has reduced to 500-600, but nevertheless the factory is still one of Tiverton's main employers. After being owned for a few years by Coats Paton the firm was bought, in 1984, by its management and still operates as John Heathcoat & Company.

Another imposing feature of the Heathcoat Amory heritage that is well known and much visited today – Knightshayes Court – was added to the local landscape in the late nineteenth century. Back in 1868 John Heathcoat Amory, on his election to parliament as one of two unopposed Liberal candidates (thus following in the footsteps of his grandfather, John Heathcoat, who had entered parliament as a Whig in 1832) wanted a new home for himself and his family. He had already (in 1866) purchased 600 acres of the Knightshayes estate – an early enclosure in the royal estate of Tiverton, north of the town – and he decided to build near the site of an eighteenth century mansion there. The architect William Burges was engaged and work proceeded in Gothic Revival style; the new Knightshayes Court was first inhabited in 1871. In 1874 John Heathcoat Amory received a baronetcy for public service. In 1914 he died, and was succeeded by his son Ian. Sir Ian

The Heathcoat lace factory, as seen in the early years of the twentieth century. The main building was destroyed by fire in 1936. (Frith)

A modern view of the Heathcoat factory. The building on the right (behind the tree) was the school provided by John Heathcoat in 1843. It now houses the factory shop. (Author)

Knightshayes Court on the outskirts of Tiverton. Built by John Heathcoat Amory in 1871, it is now in the hands of the National Trust. (Author)

died following a hunting accident in 1930 and was succeeded by the eldest of his four sons, another John. Sir John, the third baronet, married the British Women's Golf Champion Joyce Wethered in 1937. They had no children and, after Sir John died in 1972 at the age of 78, Knightshayes was left to the National Trust, in whose care it remains. His eldest nephew, Sir Ian Amory, is the present baronet and is well known in the district and county.

Largely as a result of the industrial activity, Tiverton's population rose steadily in the first half of the nineteenth century. Levels then remained fairly static for about a century before rising again by the millennium.

Population – Tiverton

1801	1851	1901	1931	1961	2001
6,505	1,144	10,382	9,610	12,397	18,621

The industrial influence continues in Tiverton, with about 20 per cent of the population currently involved in manufacturing. Besides their main factory, Heathcoats have, over the years, diversified in subsidiaries (John Heathcoat himself established enterprises abroad) and, in addition, other businesses have come in. Sadly the town no longer has its cattle market, so Tiverton on Tuesdays is not now the magnet for the scores of farmers who, within living memory, came into the town in pony traps before these were replaced by cars and trailers. The old pannier market has, however, recently been modernised and attracts many customers, and Tiverton has grown as the centre for trade and business activities for the large surrounding rural area, with wholesale and retail trade accounting for a further 20 per cent of the population. It is also a centre for business, health work, education, and administration, with the headquarters of Mid Devon District Council located in the town. The town's railway station is no more – the lines to Tiverton Junction and along the Exe valley to Exeter and to Dulverton closed in the mid-1960s – but a new station, Tiverton Parkway, has been opened on the nearby main line. Construction of the M5 motorway, completed to Exeter in 1977, and the North Devon Link Road built in the 1980s, have eased transport for commuters, both for those making inward journeys and for others who need to travel daily to Exeter or Taunton.

Such growth has caused the town's area to expand considerably, and the number of incomers continues to grow. Census figures show that migrations have come from all over England and some from Wales, while several have moved in from other parts of Devon.

Fore Street, Tiverton (now pedestrianised), looking towards the town hall which dates back to 1864. (Author)

CHAPTER THREE
Incomers for jobs and appointments

Buckfastleigh is another of the many Devon towns which in the past have been closely involved with the woollen industry. Unlike most others, however, it is a place where the industry survived until well within living memory. In fact, woollen manufacture is still represented within the parish, in the village of Buckfast, where the spinning of wool for carpets continues by the Buckfast Spinning Company, a subsidiary of Axminster Carpets.

The town, which, it is believed, dates from at least as early as the thirteenth century, really grew from the advantages of its surrounding area. With sheep abounding on the nearby slopes of south-east Dartmoor, and copious flowing streams and rivers providing water – soft for processing and swift for power – the location was perfectly set for dealing with wool, and this had been an occupation of the people from an early date. The arrival of Cistercians at the local abbey in 1147 fostered and encouraged the trade. The monks had their own woollen mill at Buckfast, worked by Dartmoor water carried by the Holy Brook, and the abbots were members of the guilds. Raw wool itself was a valuable trading commodity, involving many local people, and spinning and weaving were done by people in their homes, the unfinished cloth being taken to tucking, or fulling, mills for final treatment.

Through the centuries the industry continued at Buckfastleigh. Alongside it business also developed in the treating of skins and tanning for leather. Served by waters from the River Mardle and the Dean Burn – tributaries of the Dart – the town developed in two parts: Higher Town, close to the Mardle and the market (granted in 1353), and Lower Town, bordering Fore Street – the main thoroughfare – additionally served by the Dean Burn. The two streams join the River Dart a mile downstream from Buckfast.

Buckfastleigh was not greatly affected by the decline in the wool trade that afflicted much of Devon from the eighteenth century. Survival was assisted until 1833 by the manufacture of serge for the Chinese market, sold through the East India Company. Even after that date production continued to rise. In 1838 the small town had 700 looms – more than in any other Devon town and nearly a quarter of those remaining in the county. Up to this time the industry here had been mainly domestic, or workshop-based. Several businesses were located along Fore Street, some with the master's house fronting on to the street and the working area behind, with cottages for workers sited around a 'court'. Usually this was accessed from the street by way of an arched opening, or 'ope'.

Some of the businesses specialised in woolcombing, which had continued up to this stage by hand. New developments came in 1817 when a powered worsted spinning frame was set up at Buckfast, followed by other types of mechanical equipment. These included woolcombing machines, the coming of which drastically affected the lives of many of the townspeople. In 1850 eighteen master combers, employing 300 hand workers, who were unable or unwilling to advance to mechanisation, were put out of business.

A mill that survived well into the twentieth century was Hamlyns', located beside the Mardle in Chapel Street. Formerly the Town Mill, called Sage's, it was bought by Joseph Hamlyn in 1846. Hamlyn was also involved in a partnership that owned a nearby tannery where fellmongery (the curing of sheepskins) and wool combing were carried on. He was joined by his three sons in the business, which expanded, taking in other premises that included Buckfast's Higher Mill (the one used earlier by the Cistercians). John Berry & Company of Ashburton also established a mill at around the same time and this, too, was situated beside the Dart at Buckfast. In addition, there was a thriving iron foundry in the town, and, again beside the Dart, a papermill, both enterprises dating from the eighteenth century.

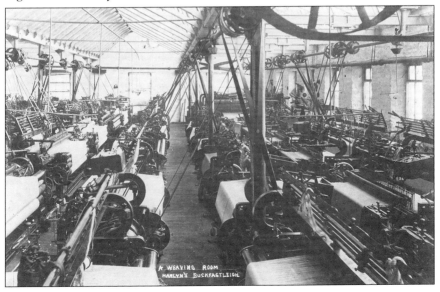

Part of the weaving room at Hamlyn's Mill, c.1900. (Author's collection)

A view from the north over the town of Buckfastleigh showing Hamlyn's woollen mill, c.1910. (From an old advert.)

A modern-day view over the redeveloped area of the former woollen mill. The large building on the right is part of the original complex. (Author)

Another Buckfastleigh woollen mill – Churchward's – was destroyed by fire on 20 April 1906. (Author's collection)

Buckfastleigh was a place of increasing activity during the nineteenth century, with around 1,000 people employed in the Town Mill alone. Not surprisingly, the population increased, reaching a peak of 2,781 by 1901, and the town acquired a distinctly industrial character. The many court cottages, and others, were inhabited mainly by families with often several members working in the mill. In 1920 Hamlyns sold the business to the Cooperative Wholesale Society, but woollen manufacture continued much as before, embracing all the skills required in textile production. The working day was punctuated by the sounding of the 'hooter' marking the times for starting and ending work at morning, noon, and evening. Meanwhile, much use was made of the railway branch to the main line at Totnes for the dispatch of goods and for bringing in the huge supplies of coal, and Buckfastleigh station presented a busy scene.

During the twentieth century much new housing development took place in and around the town of Buckfastleigh and at neighbouring Buckfast, which included the building of council estates.

By the 1970s the town's woollen industry had declined, and in 1973 the Town Mill was closed. Demolition of many of the buildings followed, and the tall chimney stack was taken down in 1976. Premises left standing were let to various small enterprises, while the fellmongery section still continued as before. Part of the cleared ground space was taken up by the erection of housing.

In many ways it appeared that a sense of quietness had descended on Buckfastleigh. For those whose lives had centred around their work at the mill, and who now rea1ised that their skills were no longer needed, it seemed as if their world had collapsed. Many of the younger people moved away, while those who stayed grew older. Despite some new developments which brought benefits, there was a general feeling that the town was 'run down'.

Prospects of new opportunities had, however, been taking shape from the late 1960s with the progress of road construction that would make the A38 a dual carriageway from Exeter to Plymouth. Some improvement for travellers had taken place in 1927 with the provision of a bypass on the south side of the town to carry through traffic away from its former route along the main street, and now that bypass was to be overtaken. For many people the idea of the new route cutting through pleasant countryside was viewed with apprehension, but it was something which, taking into account the immense growth and size of road vehicles, and the country's need for economic survival, had to be accepted. After a few years of major construction work the dualled road from Exeter to Marsh Mills at Plymouth was completed in 1976.

Nevertheless, for some years the depressed state continued. Unemployment rose to double the national average, with the highest figures in the South West, and Buckfastleigh fell into the country's top ten deprived areas. The dereliction, due to a general lack of maintenance and care, was causing many people to write off the town as beyond redemption or recovery.

The outlook for rescue seemed brighter, however, as the 1970s advanced, bringing new local government legislation. For a while Teignbridge District Council became responsible for planning, before transfer to the Dartmoor National Park Authority (DNPA), on whose south-east boundary the town is situated. From the late 1970s the DNPA focused attention on Buckfastleigh as a conservation area, a survey was conducted and plans for restoration prepared, which brought most of the town to within the prescribed category. Such definition meant that the area became eligible for grants and funding from various sources. These have included English Heritage, the Lottery, the National Trust, the Rural Development Agency (RDA), DNPA, Devon County Council, and Teignbridge District Council. In total, between three and four million pounds have been received.

Following an appraisal in 1994-5, measures were put in hand, with aid from English Heritage and other sources, to improve the appearance of the town's Fore Street which had deteriorated in recent years. The RDA

Fore Street, Buckfastleigh, as seen in the early twentieth century. (Chapman & Son, Dawlish)

Fore Street, Buckfastleigh – the modern scene. (Author)

Above and below: Two examples of the attractive 'courts' at Buckfastleigh. (Author)

financed developments around the former Town Mill site which, under new ownership, had been let in small units for individual businesses. The fellmongery, which became Devonia Products, continued in the preparation of animal skins for making rugs and leather items.

Growth of these various industries had led to an increase in both the number and size of commercial vehicles requiring access, causing constant traffic problems in the narrow Fore Street. To ease the pressure it was decided to construct a new road into the industrial side of the town from the A38, coming via Buckfast, up over Church Hill and down into the works area. This road was completed in 1999. Further changes in the shopping area followed, with the widening of pavements and the introduction of other safety measures along the now one-way street.

Meanwhile, set amidst its hills, woods and streams, Buckfastleigh gradually appeared as a convenient, unpretentious and pleasant place for living and commuting. For couples who were both working, and for single people, the abundance of former industrial housing in the town was of interesting potential. Among sought-after properties were the former workers' dwellings in the several courts, which, initially, could be acquired at reasonable cost. With suitable modernisation and updating by the new owners, these houses, although small, have taken on the aura of stylish mews residences, increasing in desirability and escalating in value. Their appearance has, in most cases, been greatly enhanced by colourful displays of potted flowering plants and window boxes, although sadly the necessity to find space for the obligatory wheely bins and recycling boxes is a slightly detracting feature. (Perhaps a solution to the problem may eventually be found.)

Needless to say, changes were not made without a degree of criticism and animosity from several of the long-established Buckfastleighites, and some such feelings still exist. Many people, however, feel the advantage of job availability from new small businesses and in catering for the greater number of visitors drawn to the various local attractions. One of these attractions, which is not new, is the former GWR branch railway line from Totnes to Buckfastleigh. Purchased privately after its closure in 1958, it is now owned by the South Devon Railway which operates a steam-driven service along the beautiful Dart valley each year from around Easter. Close to Buckfastleigh station is the Buckfast Butterfly and Dartmoor Otter Sanctuary, while in Fore Street a former public house, the Valiant Soldier, which was left in a 'time warp' after closure in the 1960s, comprises a heritage exhibition. At Buckfast the Roman Catholic Abbey church, built in the early years of the twentieth century, has long been a mecca for visitors, supplemented more recently by its large shop and restaurant.

Another fairly recent development was the relocation of the parish church. This, however, came about as the result of a traumatic event on 21 July 1992, when the town's ancient parish church on the hill, Holy Trinity, was almost totally destroyed by arson. At the time many people, especially those whose families had worshipped there for centuries, felt the loss deeply. Nevertheless, after long deliberations, and a limited amount of skilful restoration work having been carried out, it was decided that the parish church should be resited down in the town. Consequently the smaller St Luke's church, built 100 years previously as a chapel of ease, was demolished and a new, larger St Luke's erected as the parish church on the same site. Built in visionary rather than traditional style, with ancillary features befitting modern requirements, including a hall and meeting rooms, it was consecrated in 2002, and has attracted much interest from both visitors and many of the residents who see it as an icon of Buckfastleigh's future.

Buckfastleigh can no longer be said to be deprived: unemployment has considerably reduced, and wages improved; tourism has created numerous jobs, as has the proliferation of industrial units; the sheepskin business has recently been acquired by the Buckfast Spinning Company and is thus set for a wider retail market; and shops in the town have improved, although townspeople are dismayed at the recent loss of a local banking facility.

The attractions of the location and the economic upsurge have encouraged many people to move into Buckfastleigh. Population figures, which declined from the early to the mid-twentieth century rose steadily towards the millennium. The ecclesiastical parish of Buckfastleigh (which also includes the separate administrative parish of West Buckfastleigh – mainly thinly populated moorland) now has a population figure of nearly 4,000.

Population – Buckfastleigh

1801	1851	1901	1931	1961	2001
1,525	2,613	2,781	2,410	2,558	3,954

The increase, and the way in which it has happened, means that the composition of the population has greatly changed. The area's natural attractiveness, transformation of the town, and the ease of commuting, have encouraged many of the people who come to take up jobs or appointments in this sector of Devon to set up home here. Census information shows that incomers are from many counties across the stretch of southern England

and from south Wales, with smaller representations from the Midlands and the North. Of people aged 16-74 in 2001, 55.3% were in full-time economic activity (only 6% below the national average), 20% worked part-time, and 17.4% were self-employed. The highest proportion (18.5%) are involved in wholesale and retail trade, with slightly fewer in manufacturing, and health and social work, followed by education, construction, catering and business activities.

As in other places, Buckfastleigh has seen considerable increases in property values, largely due to wealth brought by incomers from other regions. For example, the court cottages, which could be acquired extremely cheaply in the early post-war years, rose to an average £35,000 by 2002, and now, amazingly, can fetch £140,000-£160,000. Whether this level can be sustained remains to be seen, but the situation, despite the improved job prospects, has certainly made matters hard for young people trying to buy a first home.

CHAPTER FOUR

Incomers for retirement

Up to the end of the eighteenth century the land surrounding Tor Bay on Devon's south coast was rural in character and generally thinly populated. With its hills and valleys, green fields and wild flowers, villages and minor roads, it would have been not greatly unlike the area farther west, around Thurlestone and Ringmore, where the South Hams descends to meet the English Channel. The northern part, which became Torquay, consisted of three ancient parishes: Cockington, St Marychurch, and Tormohun. Tormohun, named after a nearby hill (or torre) and thirteenth century Torre Abbey, had the advantage of a sheltered harbour beside which a small fish quay and several fishermen's cottages had been developed. Paignton, next along the bay, was already a town with its own small harbour. Believed to have been settled by the Saxons in the seventh century, it was a possession of the bishops of Exeter until 1644, with a bishop's palace. A market and fair were granted in 1295, and it was created a borough. Brixham, on the south side of the bay, had also been settled by the Saxons. With a harbour that formerly extended farther inland than that today, it became established over centuries as a port for fishing and boat building. Churston Ferrers, a small but ancient parish also dating from Domesday, situated just west of Brixham – between the coast and the Dart estuary – was mainly agricultural.

From the early 1800s the gentle climate and beautiful scenery of this part of England was becoming recognised, and the healthful benefits of seawater proclaimed. As a result wealthier, discriminating members of the country's population ventured west, either to visit or establish themselves and numerous impressive new homes appeared across the scene, generally sited in the best locations for enjoyment of the views. The early 'incomers' who built them either lived in them permanently – in great style, with large numbers of servants – or let them seasonally to others who came down to indulge in the natural delights. (Because this coastal location had become known for its mild winters, visitors did not come only during the summer months.) Then, in 1846, Brunel's South Devon Railway reached Newton Abbot, from where, in 1848, a branch was provided to Torre (Torquay). In 1859 the line was extended to Paignton, and in the 1860s continuation to Kingswear (for Dartmouth) enabled Brixham also to have a rail connection.

The coming of the railway made the area much more easily accessible for a wider range of people seeking rest, refreshment and pleasure, and the town of Torquay started to grow. A notable figure in its development was

Sir Thomas Palk MP, who was instrumental in establishing the still flourishing Imperial Hotel, to which many notable guests came to stay; these included, in 1877, the Prince of Wales (later King Edward VII) and his

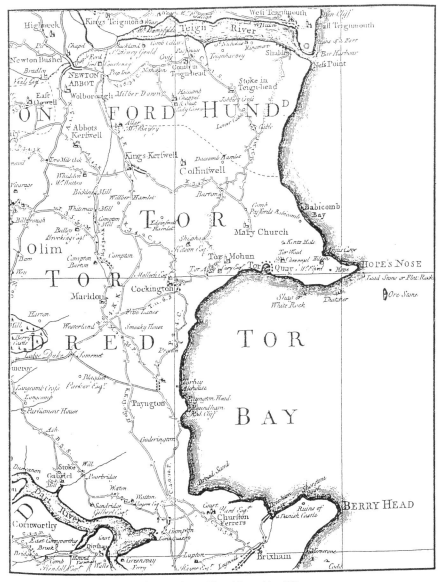

Benjamin Donn's Map of Devonshire, 1765.

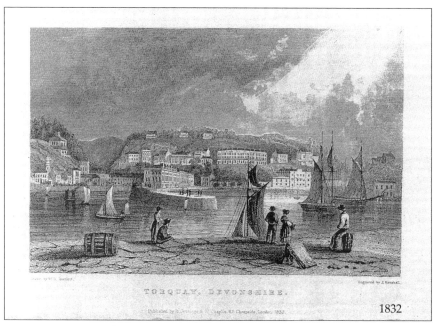

1832

(Courtesy of Westcountry Studies Library)

An engraving of the Victoria & Albert Hotel, c.1860. (Courtesy of Westcountry Studies Library)

sons. Another large, early hotel was the Victoria & Albert – now simply called the Victoria – in today's Belgrave Road. By the end of the nineteenth century Torquay had become a highly fashionable resort.

From 1900, and as the twentieth century advanced, development accelerated. With more people being able to take holidays, and with road transport also developing, increasing numbers came to Torquay as well as to Paignton, and the urban area proceeded to spread out over the countryside to accommodate them. Many of the Victorian villas were sold and became hotels, and other hotels, as well as guest houses and bed and breakfast establishments, proliferated. In addition, the towns began to acquire more popular characteristics, with growing numbers of 'attractions'.

Between the two world wars even larger numbers of people started coming to Torquay and Paignton for annual holidays, and this was a trend that continued after peace returned in 1945. Most of them took home pleasant memories from impressions gathered in summertime. Then, from the early post-war years, with the lengthening of life expectancy and the prospect of longer years of retirement to enjoy – and with pensions to finance them – many inhabitants of increasingly busy and congested parts of England remembered the golden days of holidays and headed westwards again – permanently. The Torbay area was not, of course, by any means the only one in Devon which attracted such new residents, but it is a classic example. Parts of the county have, for instance, been specially favoured by retiring members of the armed services, some of whom had already acquired homes here. Areas around Plymouth, such as Yelverton and Tavistock, are notable in this respect.

Industrial developments were also coming to the Torbay area, often as a result of firms relocating from other parts of the country. Their number must include those coming to cater for the growing tourist industry, on a large or smaller basis. It is often the case that people come in following retirement elsewhere and then re-employ themselves in providing bed and breakfast accommodation or take up part-time jobs. On the whole it is very apparent that the considerable rise in population figures in recent years is due largely to the coming in of retired people, 'keen to escape the rat race' as so many say.

Population growth and the urban spread leading to coalescence of neighbourhoods and towns prompted changes in local government in the late twentieth century. In 1969 a new County Borough of Torbay was created, incorporating Torquay, Paignton, Brixham and Churston Ferrers. Then, in 1998, in another change, Torbay became a Unitary Authority, completely independent of Devon County Council. In considering the growth figures it is therefore necessary to enumerate the separate areas in the earlier years and the combined ones later.

Population – Torbay

	1801		*1851*		*1901*
Brixham	3,671	*Brixham*	5,936	*Brixham*	8,092
Churston F.	663	*Churston F.*	786	*Churston F.*	532
Paignton	1,575	*Paignton*	2,746	*Paignton*	8,385
Tormohun	838	*Tormohun*	11,474	*Tormohun*	24,473
	--------		--------		--------
	6,747		20,942		41,482

	1931		*1961*		*2001*
Brixham	8,145	*Brixham*	10,721	*Torbay*	
Churston F.	656	*Churston F.*	1,582	*Unitary*	
Paignton	18,414	*Paignton &*		*Authority*	129,706
Torquay	46,414	*Torquay*	96,641		
	--------		--------		--------
	73,380		108,944		129,706

The population of Torbay is thus seen to have increased more than 19-fold since 1801.

Figures from the 2001 census relating to economic activity in Torbay indicate that of the 90,852 people aged 16-74, 57,530 were economically active. Analysis of this age group, expressed as percentages in comparison with those for England and Wales show:

Economic activity in Torbay – 2001 census

	Part-time	*Full-time*	*Self-employed*	*Unemployed*	*Students*
Torbay	20.5%	52.6%	17.0%	6.5%	3.4%
England & Wales	17.7%	60.9%	12.4%	5.0%	3.9%

More recently, however, statistics published by Torbay Development Agency's economic strategy unit have had disturbing effects. Figures

Torquay Harbour – the modern scene. (Author)

Torquay's Imperial Hotel, with Daddyhole beyond. (Author)

Modern developments on the east side of Torquay Harbour. (Author)

Torquay Harbour, looking towards the north-east. (Author)

showed that one in five people of working age in Torbay – 21.5% in May 2005 – were drawing benefit, and this, coupled with the fact that many of those in employment were in part-time, low paid or seasonal jobs, indicated an abnormally high number of low-income households.

Of the type of work in Torbay in 2001, the census showed that wholesale and retail trade headed the list at 18.5%, followed by manufacturing at between 14% and 15%. Not surprisingly, in an area with a relatively high level of people of advancing years, health and social work accounted for 14%. Hotels and catering showed just over 10%, followed at 8.5% by real estate, renting and business activities.

For people who retire to Torbay there is plenty to enjoy. Although much of the coastline is 'developed', there is the coastal footpath which makes accessible stretches from Maidencombe in the north, southwards to Watcombe Head, Petit Tor Point, Oddicombe and Babbacombe Beaches and Walls Hill, and to Anstey's Cove, Black Head and Hope's Nose – the northern arm of the bay. Coming around from here are the Marine Drive, with the offshore Thatcher Rock, Meadfoot Beach and Daddyhole Plain before Torquay's harbour, sea front, Torre Abbey Sands and Livermead Sands. After Hollicombe Beach and Preston Sands comes Paignton with its beach and resort features, and, south of Roundham Head, Goodrington

The north end of Paignton's sandy beach, looking across Tor Bay to Torquay. (Author)

Sands. Beyond Saltern Cove are Broadsands, Elberry Cove and the open area of Churston Golf Course, with Fishcombe Point. There is then the encounter with the urban part of Brixham, which leads out to Shoalstone Point and Berry Head. South of this are St Mary's Bay and Sharkham Point. The high ground of Berry Head, which terminates with its lighthouse, is a national nature reserve, with fine views out to sea and back across the waters of Tor Bay.

Inland, due to residential and industrial development, there is but little farming country left before the authority's boundaries with the parishes of Shaldon, Stokeinteignhead, Coffinswell, Kingskerswell, Marldon, Berry Pomeroy, Stoke Gabriel and Kingswear. But the south-eastern boundary of Dartmoor National Park is only ten miles away, which presents boundless possibilities for the many Torbay residents who enjoy walking and exploring. Within the urban area are green spaces, including the surroundings of Cockington Court, a designated country park. The sheltered sizeable harbour at Torquay also provides good facilities for those who enjoy boating and sailing – both local residents and visitors.

Besides the numerous churches, sports and arts facilities, and other attractions of interest, Torquay has an impressive and historic museum – founded in 1862 and situated in Babbacombe Road. It is owned and operated by Torquay Natural History Society and offers intellectual stimulation in programmes of talks and lectures which are very largely attended by retired people, including a high proportion of those who have settled from other places. There is also the Heritage Museum at Brixham.

Finally, one of the few drawbacks with Torbay, especially during the summer season, is that of traffic congestion. Although Torquay and Paignton are still both connected to the main railway system (the Brixham branch was closed in 1963), the majority of people – residents and visitors alike – prefer to travel by car. This, in turn, places an enormous strain on the local road system which, although improved over the years by the construction of the Torbay ring road and suchlike, has failed to keep pace with the ever-increasing demands. The A3022, where it carries traffic into and out of Brixham, is a case in point, while another – even worse – is the section of the A380 between Newton Abbot and the outskirts of Torquay. However, finding a suitable route for bypassing Kingskerswell on the A380 is proving to be a protracted business, and one that has resulted in the main access route into Torbay – the 'English Riviera' – having long since become totally inadequate.

CHAPTER FIVE
The effects

Rarely considered, perhaps, are the effects upon newcomers themselves of migrating to Devon. Most people appear to express satisfaction at their choice, although for some there must surely be certain inconveniences compared with the advantages in areas they have left, and time may be needed for making adjustments. The generally fairly mild climate is usually welcomed, although the spirits of many of those who come from drier eastern counties can be drenched by the amount of rain Devon receives. Remoteness, the very limited public transport, and complications involved in getting to the metropolis and major airports can pose problems for those accustomed to city life, especially if they have left cherished family members and friends behind.

An effect that may devolve upon members of the established population concerns housing. For many years following the Second World War this was cheap; a village house could be bought by an incomer for an apparent very reasonable sum, and money could be spent on updating improvements while still leaving buyers with cash in hand from their previous home's sale. Particularly since the millennium, however, prices have soared. Whilst this might not deter those coming from even more highly priced regions, the demands thus created by well-funded incomers have caused great difficulties for inhabitants of Devon, where twenty per cent of people in rural areas are reportedly living below the government's official poverty line, with annual incomes of less than £15,000. (Report of the Rural Advocate of the Commission for Rural Communities 2006.) The inflated prices caused by affluent purchasers have made it virtually impossible for many young Devonians to get on the first rung of the housing ladder. Despite efforts by authorities towards ensuring a proportion of 'affordable housing' there may be no alternative but to move away to less desirable areas for work, thus leading to a higher average-aged resident population and the economic and other problems this presents. Furthermore, the increasing sale of cottages and other properties for holiday or second homes compounds the problem – in some villages along the south Devon coast 40-60% of properties are occupied only in summer and sell for exorbitant prices, presenting a sad winter scene and causing detriment to the resident population who are still needed to run essential services. Land Registry figures show that in the relevant District – South Hams – the average house price in 2007 is £270,000, nearly sixteen times the average annual income here of £17,000.

The attractiveness of the county has also been seized upon by developers for the building of new estates, once planning permission is forthcoming. Parts of villages, and town fringes which formerly merged into unspoilt countryside, have, in many cases, been suburbanised. Two new towns are currently projected in Devon on present farm land. One of these, in the Sherford area east of Plymouth, is to comprise 4,000 new homes, chiefly to cater for the needs of Plymouth; the other, east of Exeter between the villages of Broadclyst and Rockbeare, to be called Cranbrook, is to provide 2,900 homes for people moving into Devon.

The following Land Registry average house price figures for January-May 2006 provide a comparison of housing prices in the four places considered in previous chapters:

Area	Detached	Semi-detached	Terraced	Flat/Maisonette	All
Bradworthy	£394,500	£140,000	--------------	------------	£309,667
Tiverton	£281,232	£164,160	£143,744	£127,211	£179,111
Buckfastleigh	£286,000	£184,333	£112,500	-----------	£206,250
Torbay	£266,851	£175,415	£147,137	£124,719	£172,484

It may be surprising to note that by far the highest average price of these four relates to Bradworthy where, as we have seen, land in the post-war years was cheap, while Torbay, which many would think of as having property of high value, is at the other end of the scale. This is partly because all housing in Bradworthy comprises detached and semi-detached houses, many of them recently built.

Devon's population is currently increasing by an estimated 5,000 a year, due to people moving in from other areas. With so many younger Devonians leaving, it is clear that Devon's face is changing as never before. What does this mean in terms of noticeable effects?

Incomers may bring an accompanying affluence and this may be reflected in raised prices for goods and services, and often in changes of appearance of neighbourhoods. Councils usually welcome new business developments to stimulate growth and, of course, to bring in more council tax. However, the increased pressure on roads, parking spaces, services and amenities may be unwelcome for those who cherish the small towns with their friendly character and locally named shops, and they may be unhappy with new anonymity and stereotyped shopping malls. Remarkably, it can often be established *newcomers* who resent undesirable changes to the towns to which they have chosen to come, and now regard as home, and who often work hard and vociferously with local societies to try to preserve valued features.

For those who care for the countryside the prospect of urban sprawl and the growth of sporadic development, as alongside roads linking towns, are causes for apprehension and concern, particularly when considering the rate of spread during the past half century. The Campaign to Protect Rural England (CPRE) is a body which works assiduously to implement its eponymous aims. In 2007 the CPRE has compiled maps showing 'tranquillity' ratings with regard to factors such as noise, scenery, open spaces and fresh air. In this, Devon is rated as the fifth most tranquil area out of 87 English counties and unitary authorities. Dartmoor and Exmoor show the county's biggest expanses of peaceful zones, while the conurbations of Plymouth, Exeter and Torbay, together with the M5 and other major roads, are the most noisy and stressful. Care must be taken that the 'in-between' land is not exploited relentlessly so that those people who live here, and those who come for peace and enjoyment of nature, do not find that the qualities they seek have been lost or destroyed. The CPRE's committees consider planning applications and, in cases that are felt to be particularly damaging to the countryside, will make formal objections, and possibly lobby the planning officers of local authorities. Generally the views of the CPRE are highly regarded.

It may take a while for incomers from London and other large cities to become accustomed to country ways. For example, some do not realise at first that when one meets another walker on a country road it is usual (with reservations) to exchange a greeting of 'Hello' or 'Good morning'. (Sometimes the newly arrived fail to reply!) Or that, when meeting another car that stops to enable passing on a narrow lane, it is customary to wave an acknowledgement – generally responded to in similar fashion. (Occasionally, however, 'locals' shamefully omit these courtesies!)

It may be amusing to spot newcomers by the way they pronounce some of our local place names. 'BUCK-FAST-LEIGH' instead of the flowing 'Buckf'stleigh' as used by established residents is a case in point. Neighbouring Totnes is sometimes incorrectly spoken of as TotNESS, and Ashburton as AshBURTON. And in west Devon, Tavistock's ancient port of Morwellham on the Tamar, now an open-air museum, is sometimes called MorWELL'am by those who do not realise that Morwell was the country estate of the abbots of Tavistock, and ham the land beside the river. Most newcomers quickly adopt and respect local ways, and thus soon become warmly accepted into the community.

Very obvious, of course, are differences of speech which are now heard throughout the county. Well-spoken regional accents are fine, and add variety and interest to conversation. One only has to listen to local radio or television for a short time to realise that many of those who participate –

interviewers or interviewees – are incomers. It would be a pity, however, if our true, warm county accent was to be submerged, or lost, and it was sad to hear of a little girl at a village school who was ostracised as 'thick' by other children because of her Devon accent. In fact, so often it is not regional speech that grates upon the ears, but what is uttered by many of today's younger people – a strange kind of stifled 'estuary' or 'media-speak' which is so unattractive and hard to understand.

Frequently it is the case that incomers bring in new energy and new ideas which stimulate activity in areas that may have acquired a certain complacency. Many are industrious and enter well into local life, contributing their skills and participating enthusiastically in town or village affairs. Churches, local history and other societies, women's institutes, sport, arts and local government may all benefit greatly from the new life coming in, and very often interested incomers acquire more knowledge about local history than those long-established.

As we look around it becomes quite clear to us that many of our very best friends are, or have been, incomers – and we certainly wouldn't want to be without them.

Index

✳ ✳ ✳ ✳ ✳